Bio

S

W9-ATY-281

BIOGRAPHY URLACHER

Brian Urlacher, Windy City
warrior

# BRIAN URLACHER

## WINDY CITY WARRIOR

SP
SPORTS
PUBLISHING
L.L.C.

ISBN 1-58261-532-2

DIRECTOR OF PRODUCTION
Susan M. Moyer

INTERIOR DESIGNER, SENIOR PROJECT MANAGER
Jennifer L. Polson

DUST JACKET DESIGNER
Kerri Baker

DEVELOPMENTAL EDITOR
Stephanie Fuqua

COPY EDITOR:
Cynthia L. McNew

Printed in Mexico.

SPORTS PUBLISHING L.L.C.
804 North Neil Street
Champaign, Illinois 61820
www.sportspublishingllc.com

# CONTENTS

# INTRODUCTION

Chicago's love affair with linebackers goes way back. In fact, many say that the Bears invented the position of middle linebacker, and Bears fans feel justifiably proud of the players in that position. Dick Butkus and Mike Singletary were dedicated, relentless foes on the field, and Brian Urlacher is definitely a player who is cast from their mold.

The Bears have won nine league championships and have been to the playoffs twenty-two times. The Pro Football Hall of Fame has enshrined twenty-four players, one coach and a general manager from the Bears, more than any other team. The pressure of living up to this legacy could be overwhelming to a new player.

But before Urlacher even set foot on Soldier Field, many predicted he was a legend in the making. And he has so far lived up to the hype. He's been to the Pro Bowl twice in two years. He was the defensive Rookie of the Year in 2000. He led the Bears that year with 125 tackles and eight sacks.

His jersey sales are the highest for any defensive player, and his management office is swamped with requests for endorsements, autographs and personal appearances. But this humble family man doesn't pay much attention to the hype and hasn't got much of an ego. He simply wants to play and play well.

Watching Urlacher on the field is to watch a dynamic player who truly loves the game. And fans of the game, not just the Bears, will truly enjoy watching him mature into the legend he's capable of becoming.

Stephanie Fuqua
Developmental Editor

# BRIAN URLACHER

## WINDY CITY WARRIOR

# Versatile Throwback

BY PETE HERRERA

**New Mexico's Brian Urlacher** is an intimidating and intriguing throwback, a cross between Chuck Bednarik and Deion Sanders.

Most of the time, the 6-foot-4, 245-pounder is a roving, roughneck free safety. But on a team with minimal talent that is struggling for a break-even season, Urlacher is much more.

He's the Lobos' go-to wide receiver in goal-line situations whose four catches this season have all been for touchdowns. He's also the team's leading punt returner, averaging nearly 11 yards a return, and he is second in scoring (30 points).

And if it were up to Urlacher and New Mexico's assistant coaches, he'd never leave the field.

"He wants to return kickoffs," head coach Rocky Long said. "And some of the coaches want him to play tailback. They come up with plays for him every week."

Urlacher, who led the nation in tackles with 178 last season, has become so valuable to the Lobos and so visible to pro scouts that his draft-day stock is soaring. Pro football analyst Mel Kiper Jr. has listed Urlacher as the seventh best prospect overall and the second best linebacker behind Penn State's LaVar Arrington.

"Usually during a season, you'll get 25 or 30 scouts come by," Long said. "We're on our second wave."

The only first-round draft pick New Mexico has ever had was linebacker Robin Cole in 1976, who went to the Pittsburgh Steelers as the 21st selection.

Tampa Bay scout Tim Ruskell said Urlacher has the speed of a defensive back and the hitting power of a linebacker.

"I was expecting to see a guy who makes a lot of plays, and he does," Ruskell said. "He's on the field almost the whole time. He's unique with a great effort level and great instincts."

Urlacher, who leads the Mountain West Conference with 107 tackles this season, is a semifinalist for the Jim Thorpe Award, which goes to the nation's top defensive back. He is also a nominee for the Bronko Nagurski Award, which recognizes the best defensive player.

He was a backup linebacker in his first two years at New Mexico under former coach Dennis Franchione. When Long came in, he moved Urlacher to safety, giving him the freedom to line up at virtually any position on defense.

That defensive scheme has helped Urlacher rack up the tackles. He had 20 at Utah last season and 20—14 unassisted—at San Diego State this year. Against San Diego State, the senior also returned a fumble 71 yards that was the difference in the Lobos' 24-21 win.

In a season-opening loss to Texas-El Paso, Urlacher recovered a fumble, forced another and caught a 20-yard pass for a touchdown. Against New Mexico State, he had 11 tackles and two catches for TDs.

"I just love being on the field," Urlacher said. "On offense, I'm always in a good situation. I score pretty much every time."

Urlacher's size and strength make it difficult for opponents to cover or tackle him. As a pass receiver, he is taller and stronger than most defensive backs. And whether returning punts or acting as a member of the Lobos' punt coverage team, Urlacher wins most collisions.

As much as he enjoys offense, he admits his passion is defense.

"I try not to gloat, but when you get a good hit, it just feels so good," he said. "You hear the crowd go 'OOH.' "

That wasn't the case during Urlacher's freshman and sophomore years at Lovington High School in southeastern New Mexico. Back then, he was a 5-foot-9, 130-pound wide receiver with speed and nothing else.

"He was just an average freshman," Lovington assistant coach Jaime Quinones said. "Nothing to indicate what the future would be like."

Through football, Urlacher and Quinones developed a friendship that remains strong. It was Quinones who got Urlacher started on a weightlifting program.

By his senior year, Urlacher had grown to 6-4 and 210 pounds. Lovington went undefeated that year, and in the state Class AAA championship game, Urlacher caught two touchdown passes, had two interceptions and forced two fumbles.

Still, New Mexico was the only Division I school to offer him a scholarship.

"If I hadn't gotten an offer, I'd probably have gone to a junior college or started working somewhere," Urlacher said. "I didn't think I was going to need college unless I was going to play football again."

After last season, he considered leaving school early to enter the NFL draft. Long and Quinones advised him to return and work on becoming a first- or second-round pick. That decision could translate into a multimillion-dollar contract.

For Urlacher, it's all a little overwhelming.

"Right now," he said, "I think $100 is a lot of money."

# Linebacker Legacy

BY THE ASSOCIATED PRESS

Clyde "Bulldog" Turner. Dick Butkus. Otis Wilson. Wilber Marshall. Mike Singletary. And someday, the Chicago Bears hope, Brian Urlacher.

The Chicago Bears took the New Mexico linebacker with the ninth overall pick in the draft, hoping he'll carry on the team's rich tradition at linebacker.

"That's the best part of being a linebacker in Chicago. All you ever hear about is Singletary and Butkus and how good they were," Urlacher said. "It's a dream come true. Hopefully, I can carry on the tradition."

Despite the team's long line of ferocious linebackers—Turner, Butkus, and Singletary are Hall of Famers—the Bears haven't had a standout at that spot since Singletary retired in 1992.

Urlacher is only the sixth linebacker the Bears have taken in the first round, and he's already projected as a starter.

"We drafted this guy because we think he's got all kinds of upside and potential," coach Dick Jauron said. "I think we're going to put him in there and let him go."

Urlacher was an All-American safety at New Mexico, where he made 422 tackles despite starting just two years. One of the most versatile players available, he also played tight end and returned kicks.

But at 6-foot-3 and 249 pounds, the Bears will play him at outside linebacker.

"I thought he could be a good safety. I think he'll be a better linebacker," Jauron said.

And while Urlacher often played two or more positions in the same game at New Mexico, he'll only play linebacker and be in the nickel defense package for the Bears.

"Asking him to play [outside] linebacker and the nickel package is a lot to ask a young man," Jauron said. "We'll concentrate on those two areas first and then move from there. At this point, I do not foresee us moving him all over the place."

Despite his size, Urlacher is quick. He was recently timed at 4.67 in the 40-yard dash. He's strong, too. He holds New Mexico's record with a 380-pound power clean, and he also squats 570 pounds.

He's a solid tackler and can shed blockers. He also has pass-rush skills, something the Bears have needed desperately the last few years.

# From Lovington to Loving Life

BY MELISSA ISAACSON

Truth be told, the coolest part of the weekend, besides getting drafted by the Bears and going to his first major-league baseball game and throwing out the first pitch for his beloved Cubs, was shopping for that truck. Just knowing that he could point his finger to the best one on the lot and drive away was, well, almost more than Brian Urlacher could bear.

So he brought his younger brother Casey along to help pick it out, to decide on all the extras—the TV and VCR and back seat that folded out into a bed for camping trips—and drive with him to his girlfriend Laurie's home in Albuquerque. And he assembled as many friends and family members as he could round up to meet him when he got there. The moment was that special.

Waiting there with the others was his stepfather Troy Lenard, though the Urlacher kids had never referred to him as either their stepdad or Troy. Brian was 11 when he met him, and he was Dad from then on. A laborer who toiled endless days in the oil fields that surround the tiny southeastern New Mexico town of Lovington, Lenard is a man who hated his job and loved his kids and never confused the two.

Brian's mom Lavoyda, Troy's ex-wife, was also there from Cleveland. So was Brian's sister Sheri, Laurie and her family, his best friend Brandon, his buddies from Lovington, and his teammates from college. Everyone he loved the most and who loved him. All were there as Brian drove up in the new truck. It was perfect.

"Boy, Brian," whistled Troy, who never had a new vehicle himself, "you're really going to love this. It's nice and roomy. It's beautiful."

"It's yours," said Brian, flipping him the keys.

Troy's reaction, said those who witnessed it, was something to see. At first he thought it was a joke. Then he refused to take the keys. Then he broke down in tears and called Brian every name in the book for doing such a thing. Then he hugged him.

"Surprise wasn't the word," said Troy. "I thought I was going to have a heart attack. Brian didn't have to do that—he knows that. It's a little too fancy for this country boy. But it's something I will cherish forever."

---

There are only so many things to know about Brian Urlacher to really get the picture, and it would be easy to mistake most of those things as hokey. But then that would be missing the point. To call him sentimental and wholesome and more than a little bit corny, however, would not offend him in the least.

For fun on Friday nights in Lovington, Urlacher and Brandon Ridenour, who made a pact never to drink alcohol in high school, would "cruise up and down the main street, drinking chocolate milk," said Urlacher. "Unless it was Friday night during football season; then we'd have a dance."

The night he returned from Chicago, where the Bears made him the ninth pick in the NFL draft—a distinction that will earn him a first contract somewhere in the neighborhood of $8 million, not counting his signing bonus—Urlacher had dinner with friends at a drive-in. Then he played miniature golf.

"We went to Panama City, Fla., for spring break," said Ridenour, "and we played miniature golf four or five times. No one believed us."

If it's not miniature golf, it's bowling. If it's not bowling, it's ping-pong. "He has his own paddle," said Ridenour, "and he carries it around in his car just in case he needs it. He's convinced he's the best ping-pong player in the world."

He's also pretty sure he has a future in pro wrestling if he so desires, what with 20-some years of experience leaping on his brother's back, ambushing Ridenour, and wrestling on the floor with every friend he has ever had.

Then there are the other games. The hours of paper-rock-scissors with his New Mexico football road roomie Rantie Harper, who sheepishly asks you to trust him that it was in the spirit of competition. The bed-jumping contests and peanut fights with Harper and

linebacker Mike Barnett and eventually the rest of the team. The game in which the first guy names an athlete and the next has to use the first letter of the last name and come up with the next player in the same sport until you run out of sports and bus rides.

"Everyone was always in our room, playing all these crazy games," said Harper. "And what it really was, was Brian. Whatever he did, everyone just wanted to be around him."

---

Born May 25, 1978, in Pasco, Wash., and weighing in at 11 pounds 8 ounces, Brian Keith Urlacher arrived a year and 10 days after his sister Sheri and just short of 15 months before his brother Casey.

Lavoyda Beeman was 16 when she married high school beau Brad Urlacher and had three children by the age of 19. Divorced by 25, she took her kids and followed her parents back to New Mexico, where she had once lived.

"She's an incredible woman," said Brian, referring to those first few years in Lovington. At one point, she worked three jobs to keep the family afloat: a 6-10 a.m. shift at an automated laundry, followed by a 2-10 p.m. shift as a grocery store checker, and then an 11 p.m.- 5:30 a.m. shift at a convenience store. With breaks in between to shuttle the children to and from school and games, understanding bosses who allowed her kids to sit in back rooms and do their homework, baby-sitting help from her parents, and occasional shifts off to sleep, she kept that schedule going for close to a year. Then she reduced the workload to two jobs.

"That was just until we got back on our feet," she said. "We ate a lot of macaroni and cheese during that time, but the kids never went without. I had energy and desire, and I swore we were going to make it one way or another."

Brian was a quiet, skinny kid, the classic middle child. They called him "Mr. Clean" because of his aversion to dirt, and even after finding his passion for football in the 6th grade, no one was predicting he would start at linebacker for the Chicago Bears.

In Lovington, Brian and Casey played on a bucking barrel used to simulate bull riding and became addicted to the Cubs. "Because we could watch them on TV," he said. "It was either the Cubs or soap operas."

In Little League, playing for opposing teams, the brothers' competition deepened. Once, with Brian pitching and Casey batting, Brian plunked his little brother. "He had doubled against me in his last at-bat, so I hit him," Urlacher said by way of explanation. "He wasn't mad."

"I just smiled at him," said Casey, "and ran to first."

As the Urlacher kids grew, so did their family. When their mother married Troy Lenard in 1992 after a three-year courtship, the boys slept three to a room, sharing with Lenard's son David. "A lot of times they didn't have the things they wanted, but we always managed," said Lenard. "We had a lot of good times. It makes me want to sob, I'm so proud of all of them."

Brian pauses when he speaks of Lenard, the man his mother said is "the only father he ever knew."

"He was a great role model, a hard worker, a great friend," he said. "He gave us something to strive for."

That is, as long as that something was anything but the fields that produce a good portion of the nation's crude oil where Brian occasionally worked summers. "We maintain the oil fields, sometimes 24 hours a day, sometimes 10," Lenard explained.

"I've always told my boys to pursue schooling, to make life easier for themselves than I did. It's no life for anyone."

---

For Brian, focusing on school and sports came naturally. In the classroom, he earned mostly As and Bs. And in football, after unspectacular freshman and sophomore seasons, he began to blossom.

He became a student of the game, spending extra hours in the film room studying opponents, and he discovered the pain and reward of weight training.

"Brian lived in that weight room," said Lovington's defensive coordinator, Jaime Quinones, whom Brian still calls Coach Q. "And he never questioned anything you told him to do."

As a senior, he was voted Mr. Lovington High School, averaging 20 points and 11 rebounds on the basketball team and leading the football team to the Class 3A state title as a wide receiver, strong safety, punt and kick returner and flier on the punt-return team.

"On offense, our philosophy was basically just to get the ball to him," said Quinones. "You could just throw it up, and he'd jump and dominate."

On defense and on punt returns, opponents tried to avoid him, a practice that continued at New Mexico.

"If you were standing around with Brian on the field, you were going to get laid out," Quinones said. "His junior year, we had to talk to him about it because it was borderline [legal]. He just loved contact."

Off the field, Urlacher loved working with the kids in Quinones's special-education classes, which he did on a voluntary basis. "I had one boy Brian's age who really needed special attention, and Brian just jumped right in," Quinones recalled. "It was the first period of the day and Brian was always there, playing ball with him, talking to him. He did that the whole year for me."

Urlacher called it one of the highlights of high school. "They call it Down syndrome, but those kids are so happy, such a joy to be around," he said. "I loved working with them."

Only once does anyone remember Urlacher getting in trouble. Seems

a high school math teacher accused Urlacher and a friend of swiping the answers to a test.

"They kept denying it, but we were pretty well convinced they did it," said Lovington High Principal and Athletic Director Art Karger. "So we gave each of them two swats."

The "Brian" part of this incident is that he never held a grudge. He and Karger remain close, and today, Karger's youngest son Bryce is an associate of his agent, Steve Kauffman. "He wasn't going to let something like that ruin our friendship," said Karger. "He knew it wasn't personal."

Not long ago, Urlacher gave Karger an autographed picture for his office. He signed it, "Thanks for the beating, Brian Urlacher."

"Just recently," said Karger, "he told me, 'I swear to you, I didn't take that book.'"

---

If Urlacher were a bitter man, he could start with the rejection of Texas Tech, the one school where he really wanted to play. Tech told him he could try to walk on. He could also resent all the other schools that ignored him, which would include every Division I college but New Mexico and a good share of Division II and Division III schools that should have known better.

Poised to work and attend a junior college near home, his future finally took hold when New Mexico coaches came calling on the 6-foot-3-inch, 200-pounder they made into a linebacker. Over the next four years, playing safety, linebacker, receiver, tight end, and special teams, Urlacher made them look brilliant.

"I'm just glad someone found me," he said. "The chance that I got from New Mexico was a blessing."

Until his junior year, he said, the thought of playing in the NFL barely occurred to him. The summer before, Lenard first noticed the physical burst. During college, Urlacher added 40 pounds of muscle.

"He came home," said Lenard, "and I asked him, 'What happened to your neck? It looks like your head is sitting right on your shoulders.'"

In his junior year, Urlacher led the nation with 178 tackles from a hybrid free safety spot that allowed him to roam the field and hone in on the ball. After the season, he told head coach Rocky Long he was considering leaving school early for the NFL draft.

"I did some research for him and told him that he'd probably go anywhere from the fifth to the seventh round," said Long. "I said, 'Brian, if you go in the fifth round, you'll probably get a $40,000 to $50,000 signing bonus. If you wait and go in the first round, you'll make a million or two.'

"He said, 'Coach, $40,000 or $50,000? That's a lot of money.'"

Urlacher's friends and family joke that it still seems a fortune to him. His agent, Kauffman, said his new client did not want to speak about his future contract until after the draft. Now he wants to focus on mini-camp this weekend. Undoubtedly, then it will be Platteville in July.

"I don't think he really grasps how much money he's going to have," said his friend Ridenour. "That's not what he's about. He knows he'll have enough to do some stuff with, have a nice car, take care of his family. That's it."

Urlacher laughs when asked about arriving in Chicago the Saturday night of the draft in the same jeans and half-buttoned, by-then rumpled shirt he had on that morning.

"I didn't have time to change, and I didn't even think about it," he said. "I do have a suit though. I had to buy it for an ESPN awards show. I went to Lovington and got it on sale, half off, so it was a good deal."

Girlfriend Laurie Faulhaber tells of Bears executives asking Brian if he was hungry the night they arrived. "Sure, why don't we drive through McDonald's?" he replied.

The next day they told him to be sure to order whatever he wanted from the room service menu. "He ordered chicken tenders," laughed Faulhaber. "I was like, 'Brian, you can't come up with anything better than that?' He said, 'But chicken tenders sound good.'"

---

Urlacher is already planning his move to Chicago. Besides Faulhaber and the couple's two basset hounds and one 23-pound cat, he wants Casey, a linebacker at New Mexico Military Institute, to move in with him and try to walk on at a school within driving distance.

"I want to be closer to him," said Casey, who will have his tuition paid for by his big brother. "I'd like to watch him play and he'd like to watch me. I really couldn't ask for more in a brother. I'm so proud of him."

Urlacher is also trying to talk Ridenour, who will be a senior on the Eastern New Mexico basketball team, into spending the summer. And his mother and sister, who now live in Cleveland, where his mother does data entry for American Coffee Services, are thrilled about the relatively short commute.

"When he left for Chicago," said Lavoyda, "he picked me up and hugged me, and he said, 'Well, Mom, it's time for me to do my real job now.' It about broke my heart."

He does have that effect on people. After his last college game, he found Coach Q in the stands and gave him his helmet. Against the advice of many, Urlacher left Mobile, Ala., two days before the Senior Bowl to attend New Mexico's senior banquet, arriving back in the wee hours the morning of the game in which he was named his team's most valuable player.

**When he left for Chicago, he picked me up and hugged me, and he said, 'Well, Mom, it's time for me to do my real job now.' It about broke my heart.**

**—Lavoyda Lenard, Brian's mother**

"I don't think he thought it was necessary to come back," said Long. "For our seniors it's a big deal, and more important, for his teammates it was a big deal that he was there with them. That's the kind of person he is."

"That's just Brian" is the common refrain. "He just gives and gives and gives," said Casey.

To this day, when the Urlacher brothers end a phone conversation, it's, "Bye, Brian, love you. Love you too, Casey."

"I know it seems corny," said his girlfriend, "but he's just a great big ol' kid who loves his friends and his family and sports. That's just Brian."

# Signed to a Five-Year Deal

BY THE ASSOCIATED PRESS

**The Chicago Bears signed** first-round draft pick Brian Urlacher to a five-year contract Friday.

The signing means that for the first time in three years, the Bears will have their No. 1 draft pick when summer training camp opens in July.

"I'm pretty excited," Urlacher said. "I got signed a lot sooner than a lot of people thought. . . . I'm glad because I wanted to be in camp."

He added: "Everyone is down on you if you don't go to camp. You're behind. It hurts you and the team."

In 1998, running back Curtis Enis missed four weeks and had a disappointing rookie year. Last season, quarterback Cade McNown missed two weeks of camp.

"Knowing that Brian's going to be in camp on time is a big deal for us," Bears coach Dick Jauron said. "We've already said he's going to be the starting strongside linebacker, and he'll be there from day one."

Terms of the agreement were not disclosed.

# Urlacher Loses Starting Job

**BY THE ASSOCIATED PRESS**

**All the praise in the world** couldn't help Brian Urlacher remain a starter for the Chicago Bears.

Urlacher was replaced in the starting lineup by Rosevelt Colvin after Tuesday's practice.

"It's because I didn't play very well and Rosie was playing better," Urlacher said Wednesday before ducking an approaching media swarm.

The Bears named Urlacher as a starter on the strong side almost immediately upon drafting him out of New Mexico, where he seemed to play all over the field. A roving safety and occasional linebacker in college, Urlacher even caught six touchdowns on seven receptions as a receiver in 1999. He also returned kicks.

His freakish athletic ability was one reason he was coveted.

Bears coach Dick Jauron said he didn't regret handing Urlacher a starting job before playing one snap in camp.

"It's a new position, it's a new league, and that was the easiest linebacker position to learn," Jauron said. "But I won't second-guess myself."

Urlacher still might be the next great Bears linebacker, following Dick Butkus and Mike Singletary, but he's going to have to work his way back into the starting lineup first.

Jauron said Urlacher would still see plenty of playing time, mostly in nickel and dime packages.

"Brian will still get on the field in situations, we'll make sure of that," Jauron said. "He's too good an athlete not to. He's not going to be watching the whole game."

Urlacher attended all mini-camps and avoided progress-stunting contract holdouts like those of recent Bears No. 1 draft picks, Cade McNown and Curtis Enis.

But starting immediately was too much for him, defensive coordinator Greg Blache said.

"We were force-feeding a kid an elephant and you saw him choke a little bit. When that happens, you're gonna give the kid the Heimlich maneuver," Blache said. "He should be a fine football player, but there's no sense in killing the guy and breaking him before you get started."

But Blache said naming Urlacher as starter before camp did not hurt the rookie.

"It didn't stunt his development. It made him take a crash course," Blache said.

# Interception Preserves Win

**BY RICK GANO**

**All season long,** Brian Urlacher's instincts have outweighed his experience, his raw skills compensating for a rookie's on-the-job training.

Urlacher will be the first to tell you he still doesn't have it all figured out, but his feel for the game and his teammates has improved every week.

"I started out poorly, so I'm glad both the fans and my teammates are starting to accept me more. It's important to me," Urlacher said Sunday when his late interception preserved the Chicago Bears' chilly 13-10 win over Tampa Bay.

Urlacher's interception was one of two by the Bears against Shaun King. Tony Parrish made one near the end of the first half, returning it 38 yards for a touchdown as Urlacher delivered an earth-shattering block to flatten 340-pound Bucs tackle Jerry Wunsch during the runback.

"We're starting to figure out where we are supposed to be and how we are going to help each other. We feel that it's building," said Urlacher, the Bears' first-round pick.

Bears defensive tackle Mike Wells said Urlacher, the team's leading tackler, is getting better.

"He'll say, 'I made a play because of what you guys did,'" Wells said. "But most of the time, he'll do it by himself."

# Surprised at Special Teams Honor

BY NANCY ARMOUR

**It was nearly impossible** to watch TV on Sunday night without seeing a replay of Brian Urlacher's first NFL touchdown catch.

But he never saw this coming.

The Chicago Bears linebacker was named the NFC's special teams player of the week after scoring the game-winning TD on a fake field goal in Sunday's 20-15 victory in Washington.

"Me?" Urlacher said when told about the award. "Wow."

Good thing Urlacher wasn't the one handing out the awards, because he would have given it to punter Brad Maynard.

"That's cool, I guess, but I think Brad should have gotten it," he said.

Trailing 13-10 early in the fourth quarter, the Bears had lined up for what looked like a field goal. Instead Maynard, normally the holder on field goals, threw a pass to Urlacher, who played a little receiver at New Mexico.

The Redskins were caught off guard—even after Urlacher went in motion—and Urlacher waltzed into the end zone untouched for the 27-yard score.

The award makes Urlacher the first NFC player to be recognized in two different categories since 1996, when Green Bay's Don Beebe won offensive and special teams honors. Urlacher won NFC defensive player honors after Week Four, when he returned a fumble 90 yards for a touchdown and had a sack.

Urlacher is the mainstay of Chicago's defense, leading the Bears with 131 tackles. He also has five sacks and three interceptions. But with his freakish speed and sure hands, there's been talk of him playing some offense since he arrived in Chicago.

His senior year at New Mexico, he caught seven passes—six for touchdowns. Just last week, offensive coordinator John Shoop said he'd love to put Urlacher in a receiver's jersey and see what he could do.

But Urlacher is quite happy doing what he's doing, thank you.

"It was fun to have the ball thrown my way, but I'm not going to try and get out there and do any more," he said. "If they need me, I will. If they want me out there, I will. But I'm not going to push it."

# Not Caught Up in the Hype

BY NANCY ARMOUR

Chicago Bears linebacker Brian Urlacher was on the phone with his high school coach one Sunday night, talking about friends, families, and the hometown news like they always do in their regular chats.

Eventually, the subject got around to that day's game in Buffalo, and Jaime Quinones asked how Urlacher did.

"He said, 'Oh, Coach, I did OK.' Then come to find out, he had 16 tackles," Quinones said, laughing. "He's very humble. He's not going to brag about himself."

Picked ninth overall in last spring's draft out of New Mexico, Urlacher has been one of the few bright spots for the woeful Bears (4-11). Already drawing comparisons to Dick Butkus and Mike Singletary, he leads the Bears in tackles, sacks, and fumble recoveries and is second in interceptions. A first alternate to the Pro Bowl, he's the favorite to win defensive Rookie of the Year honors.

But don't expect him to tell you about any of that.

"I just don't like calling attention to myself. It's a team sport," he said. "I think I've always been brought up to be a humble person, knowing that I can still do things better."

That Urlacher landed in Chicago is almost too perfect. The Bears were "The Monsters of the Midway," with tough linebackers like Butkus, Singletary, Otis Wilson, Clyde "Bulldog" Turner, and Wilber Marshall.

And despite its brokerage houses downtown and upscale shops on Michigan Avenue, Chicago remains a working-class city, blue-collar to the core. Urlacher is a guy who can relate.

Growing up in Lovington, a town of about 9,000 in the southeastern corner of New Mexico, Urlacher can't remember a summer when he didn't have a job. His stepfather, Troy Lenard, worked in the oil fields, and his mother, Lavoyda, sometimes juggled two and three jobs.

Urlacher himself worked oil pipeline construction the summer before he went away to college, toiling 12 hours a day in 100-degree heat for $7 an hour.

"I've been brought up that if you want to get something, you're going to have to work for it. There's no other way to get it," he said. "No one's going to give you anything. That's just the way I live my life."

He hasn't gotten caught up in the trappings of his newfound success and wealth, either. There are no chunky gold chains around his neck, no diamonds in his ears. He doesn't make the gossip columns or hang out at the best parties.

He and his wife, Laurie, live in a northern suburb with their newborn daughter and his younger brother, Casey. There's a ping-pong table in the basement.

His big-ticket purchase? Casey's tuition at Lake Forest College.

"I told him before I even got drafted that wherever I went, I wanted him to come with me. I just feel comfortable with him around, he's one of my best friends," Urlacher said of his brother, who is 15 months younger.

"It's always good to have someone around that you love and loves you back and you can have a good time with. My wife is the same way."

Snubbed by every Division I school but New Mexico and a backup until his junior year when coach Rocky Long arrived, Urlacher is well aware that he owes some of his success to the people who've supported him along the way.

It's why he calls Quinones every other week. Why he's on the phone with the New Mexico football office at least once a week, talking with anyone who is available. Sometimes it's Long, sometimes defensive coordinator Bronco Mendenhall, sometimes a secretary.

And if New Mexico wins a game it wasn't expected to, Long knows he can expect a call from Urlacher.

"I owe them a lot, and I think I realize that," Urlacher said. "And those are great guys. Those are the people that shoot you straight. They don't like you because of what you are or who you are, they like you because of the person you are. They've been my friends forever."

As he gets better, the spotlight on him and the demands that go along with it grow. While most teams put their quarterback or marquee offensive player on the weekly conference calls with out-of-town media, Urlacher gets the duty for the Bears.

His jersey is already a best-seller in Chicago, with little kids running around Soldier Field wearing No. 54.

All of this, and he hasn't scratched the surface of his potential.

"I think he doesn't get caught up in it because he knows one day it could be all over with," Casey Urlacher said. "He's just enjoying it and having fun right now, and that's the way it should be, a lot of fun instead of so much of a business.

"He's doing good for himself, being 22, so I'm really proud of him."

# Winning Top Rookie Honors

BY NANCY ARMOUR

The scariest thing about Chicago Bears linebacker Brian Urlacher isn't his speed. Or his vicious hits that can be heard way up in the stands. Or how he comes out of nowhere to lay a quarterback flat on his back.

The scariest thing is that he's only going to get better.

"He's playing on emotions right now, a love for the game . . . he's just playing on that instinct," Bears defensive end Bryan Robinson said. "And he has great instincts. Just imagine once he gets the true technique and the true factors of playing football, he's going to be a good one."

Urlacher is already pretty good. He picked up The Associated Press Defensive Rookie of the Year award Sunday, easily winning it with 27 1/2 votes from the nationwide panel of 50 media members.

New Orleans end Darren Howard was second with 15 1/2 votes, and Philadelphia Eagles tackle Corey Simon was third with six. Cleveland Browns end Courtney Brown, the No. 1 pick, got the other vote.

Though he's a first alternate to the Pro Bowl, Urlacher was stunned when told of the honor. He figured Howard or Simon had Rookie of the Year locked up. Howard led all rookies with 11 sacks, and Simon was second with 9 1/2.

Plus, the Saints and Eagles made the playoffs, while the Bears (5- 11) are settled into their couches, remote controls in hand, with nothing to do but watch TV.

"It's amazing. I'm so happy," Urlacher said. "I was pretty sure I wouldn't get it just because we didn't have a very good record. I guess not. I guess I played well enough."

That's one way to put it. Urlacher didn't even start the first two games, yet still led the Bears with 125 tackles and eight sacks. He also had two interceptions and a fumble recovery.

He was one of the few bright spots in a dismal season for the underachieving Bears and their fans. Flying around the field, delivering hit after hit, he gave fans something to cheer about every time he took the field.

Take his game at Buffalo, where he was in on 16 tackles. Or the game against Tampa Bay, when he delivered a bone-crunching block on 340-pound Buccaneers tackle Jerry Wunsch to help clear the way for Tony Parrish's interception return, and then picked off a pass on his own to seal the victory.

"Brian Urlacher is a playmaker," Bears coach Dick Jauron said. "He can make a difference in a game."

Compared to Dick Butkus and Mike Singletary since he was drafted, Urlacher has already topped the Hall of Famers in one respect—neither Butkus nor Singletary earned Rookie of the Year honors. Tackle Wally Chambers (1973) and safety Mark Carrier (1990) are the only other Bears players who won the award.

"You only get a chance to win Rookie of the Year once," Urlacher said. "It means a lot."

The Bears knew they were getting a great athlete when they took Urlacher with the ninth pick. He'd played free safety, linebacker, tight end, and receiver at New Mexico and also returned kicks.

They wanted him on the field right away, so they made him the starter at outside linebacker, figuring it was the easiest position to learn. But Urlacher struggled in training camp, eventually losing his starting job before the final preseason game.

"I didn't know what to expect coming into this year," he said, "and then I started out so bad with training camp and it was really frustrating."

But when middle linebacker Barry Minter got hurt in the second game, Urlacher went in, and he's never come out. Though middle linebacker is tougher to learn than strong-side and requires him to call signals for the defense, it's more like the rover position he played at New Mexico.

## You only get a chance to win rookie of the year once. It means a lot.

### —Brian Urlacher

In his first start, against the New York Giants, he had 13 tackles and his first sack.

"I think I got better and better as the season went on," he said.

And he'll get better still, Minter said.

"The sky is the limit right now for him," Minter said. "He's still scraping the barrel on learning how to play linebacker. Right now, he's doing still a lot of things on straight talent and ability.

"You will probably see a different, more improved Brian Urlacher next year. With a year here working in the system, in the weight room, watching some film in the off season, he'll be even better next year."

# Homecoming King

**BY MELISSA ISAACSON**

**They had to be a little worried.** Last time home, after all, he was still just Brian. Neither a Pro Bowler nor a millionaire. Not yet a father, or even a husband, for that matter. Certainly not a big-time, Nike-sponsored, khaki-wearing Chicago guy who just walked onto the set of a national sports network the other week and started chatting up the hosts like he actually knew them and they him.

They all saw that. Couldn't believe it was their Brian. Saw the Pro Bowl, too, of course. And most Bears games, courtesy of an attorney in town who opened his office and his satellite feed to whoever wanted to drop in and watch Lovington's own Brian Urlacher upend and level unsuspecting opponents.

The Lovington High School football team, decked out in their new sweats and cleats courtesy of their most famous alum, watched highlights of his big hits all season. And not just his NFL hits, but his Lovington hits, collected on a '95 Wildcats highlight film, since dubbed the "Brian highlight film."

They were all there Saturday night. The Lovington football players, past and present. The coaches from grade school through college. His 7th-grade algebra teacher selling tickets to raffle off his signed Bears jersey. His mom Lavoyda and sister Sheri from Louisiana; brother Casey, an all-conference middle linebacker at Lake Forest College; their stepdad Troy, now living outside Dallas.

And a high school gym full of people who either had a brother who played with Brian or a spouse who was in his homeroom; friends of his parents; a cop who coached him; or a cousin of a cousin who had Thanksgiving dinner with him once.

The call went out in the building for someone who did not actually know Brian Urlacher on a personal or semi-personal basis, and a woman came running with her discovery.

"I found a family who doesn't know him at all," she said excitedly. "They're visiting from Brazil. But they don't speak English."

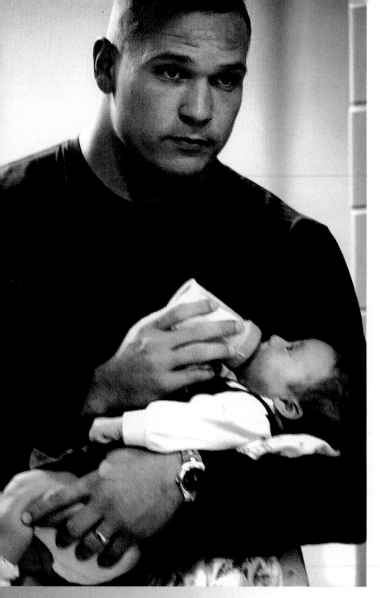

The kindly older gentleman at the rental car counter in nearby Hobbs, home of the Wildcats' rivals who have recently riled Lovington folks by claiming Urlacher as a fellow Lea County resident, did not know Brian. But he felt like he did and wished he could have scored a few tickets to Brian Urlacher Night.

"We're so glad you're here," he said to visitors who informed him they were from Chicago. "It's so thoughtful of you to come all this way for Brian. He's such a wonderful young man."

The rental agent wished he could be of more help, such as offer a better answer when one of the visitors asked what there was to do in the area. But, alas, these are honest people.

"Nothing," he said pleasantly, pointing the way.

"It's the same way as when I left it," said Urlacher, who was last here close to a year ago. "That's why I like it. It will always be the way I left it."

There are the coffee shops and the old courthouse and the Sonic drive-in just off Main Street, where Urlacher and best buddy Brandon Ridenour would cruise in Brian's 1978 Chevy Luv or Brandon's shockless Dodge Shadow, gulping chocolate milk out of the carton.

But there's also the McDonald's and Burger King, one of the most blatant signs of progress in Lovington and a source of irritation for Urlacher, whose first meal after signing his first pro contract, complete with a check for a $5.5 million signing bonus, was at McDonald's.

"After I went to college, we get a McDonald's," he said with disgust. "It [stinks]."

Otherwise, this desert town of 9,500 in southeastern New Mexico, still rebounding from the oil crisis in the mid-'80s, is known more for the 17,000 rigs that surround it. And for a small-town familiarity and humble stock that still remembers a time not too long ago when no prefix was necessary, just five numbers to dial your friends or relatives.

And now, of course, for a homegrown kid who has made them proud.

"It gives us all a sense of pride," said Josh Faith, son of Lovington High head football coach Speedy Faith. "It lifts the whole town up because he's a Lovington product. It makes us all feel good. It shows us that dreams really do come true, and that if you set your mind to it, you can do anything."

As a show of appreciation, they brought him back scarcely five years after he led the football team to an undefeated season and state championship to honor him. "I can't believe they did it so soon," said Urlacher, as if he needed more credentials than being a first-round draft choice, Pro Bowler, and NFL Defensive Rookie of the Year.

Packing about 3,000 townspeople into the gym for the 30-minute ceremony during halftime of Saturday night's basketball game, they made Urlacher the first inductee enshrined in the Lovington Hall of Fame, presented him with a plaque commemorating his achievements from the New Mexico House of Representatives, and retired his basketball and football jerseys.

Walking onto the court beside wife Laurie and cradling 2-month-old daughter Pamela, Urlacher blushed as his high school coach wept and fathers in the bleachers hoisted children in Bears jerseys to get a better glimpse.

Finally, Urlacher's brother and sister unfurled the No. 11 banner that would be hoisted above the court. "Brian," intoned school superintendent Art Karger as the crowd fell quiet, "no one will ever wear this jersey again."

"If kids can't draw inspiration from him," said Jaime Quinones, a Lovington assistant football coach, "they're missing something."

If there was a rallying cry to Urlacher's return home, that was it. In the wake of a Super Bowl in which the MVP's implication in a double murder last year was the central theme, the town of Lovington clings to a hero they are confident will never bring them shame.

"You can attach yourself to Brian and feel secure he's not going to do something that would embarrass his town or his family," Karger said.

"That's a big thing," said city manager Bob Carter.

If Urlacher so much as taunted an opponent, he said, he would expect a phone call.

"I know if I ever said or did something stupid," said Urlacher, whose signature move after a big hit or sack this season was a wide smile, "every one of those people would be calling and saying, 'What were you thinking?'"

He says he has "grown up" in the last year, that getting married and having a baby at 22 has settled him down.

"But I don't really feel any different," he said. "I feel happier. I have my

**But I don't really feel any different. I feel happier. I have my daughter and my wife and everything's going good, but I still feel the same. I'm sure people look at me differently, but I'm still the same dude.**

**—Brian Urlacher**

daughter and my wife and everything's going good, but I still feel the same. I'm sure people look at me differently, but I'm still the same dude."

Pamela Urlacher, who traveled with her parents to Honolulu for the Pro Bowl, has not overwhelmed her young parents, her father says, but rather transformed them.

"It's amazing, just unbelievable how much happiness she can bring to your life," he says. "I can stare at her all day because she makes so many different faces and now she's starting to smile. She has those gums showing and she's so cute. Every day gets better. Just hanging out with her and my wife, I'm not missing anything in life right there."

The implication this NFL season, as it became more and more obvious that Urlacher was one of the best linebackers in the game, was that the rookie could take his place beside Dick Butkus and Mike Singletary; that the only thing holding him back was an inferior team around him.

"Brian really didn't like that," said Casey Urlacher. "You can't compare him to those players yet."

Urlacher admitted that dealing with the media "overwhelmed me. They always wanted to talk to me and I could never figure out why," he said with apparent sincerity.

Though friends railed back home, dropping him out of the starting lineup for the first two games of the season was the right thing to do, Urlacher said, though his brother says he was so despondent about the move that he didn't tell him about it for two days.

"If they had put me at [middle linebacker] at the beginning," he said, "I don't think I would have done well because I didn't know the calls. I had never called a defense before and I think I just would've been nervous and the guys would've gotten on me and yelled at me because I would be screwing up.

"As a rookie, your self-esteem gets lowered, your confidence goes down . . . .

"They knew what they were doing."

The whirlwind nature of a year that started with the NFL combine and never slowed is just beginning to hit him, he said. Newfound wealth has brought with it a

**We are all living Brian's dream right now. But he can make twice as much money as he's making now and to me, he's still the same kid. He's just Brian and I don't want him to change.**

**—Troy Lenard, Brian's stepfather**

new house equipped with his dream basement.

"Ping-pong, air hockey, pool, darts, shuffleboard, video games—it's very nice, but I'm still working on it," he said. "Growing up and seeing how athletes would have these great game rooms, that was a goal of mine."

Urlacher still does not own a car, but he did purchase six new vehicles for his wife, mother, stepdad, brother, sister and Brandon. He also bought his stepdad, whom the Urlacher children have only known as Dad since their mother married him in '92, a three-bedroom home sitting on 112 acres complete with two fishing ponds in Rising Star, Texas.

"He retired me," said Troy Lenard. "He wanted me to come see a game and I couldn't get off work, so he told me to quit. Two days later, I was sitting in the rain in Soldier Field watching the first pro game I ever saw.

"We are all living Brian's dream right now. But he can make twice as much money as he's making now and to me, he's still the same kid. He's just Brian and I don't want him to change."

# The Time of His Life

BY MELISSA ISAACSON

**Every time Brian Urlacher** was caught on camera between plays last season, the Bears' rookie linebacker seemed to be laughing uproariously.

While NFL defenders—former Bears linebacker Bryan Cox springs immediately to mind—have been known to concoct motivational scenarios in which the men trying to stop them from maiming a ballcarrier are really brutal maniacs who attacked their wives or girlfriends, Urlacher has always treated a crushing hit like a good punch line.

Imagine his giddiness now that it's all coming much easier to him. "I'm just reacting now," he says. "I know where I'm going. It just makes so much more sense to me. It's so much more fun."

So much more that Urlacher has been treating his improved skills with the same sort of spirited recklessness as a kid with a new GameBoy.

"Honestly, right now my biggest problem with Brian is that he's gotten so much better, he wants to start guessing," says defensive coordinator Greg Blache. "I told him he has to call [the psychic] Miss Cleo before he comes to practice. Where he's getting in trouble, he's trying to go somewhere too fast, and he's guessing where it's going to go before it happens because he's that comfortable and confident....

"But he's having fun and doing a great job of guessing."

With the exception of a recent afternoon off with a strained lower back, Urlacher navigates the fields of Platteville with a joy that is clearly infectious. One day recently, however, was a bad one for Urlacher.

"In one day, Pamela crawled two steps, her front teeth came in, and she ate a whole jar of sweet potatoes. She just had a huge day and he was really sad he missed it," says wife Laurie Urlacher.

Dad confirms this as his face reddens. "I was so mad I missed her teeth come through," he says, as if somehow he could have caught the moment on videotape. "She was just born yesterday and now she's practically all grown."

More than anything, Brian and Laurie agree, this is what defines him now.

"My favorite story," she says, "is when he was [signing autographs] in New Orleans and someone walked up to him and said 'Congratulations.' And Brian said, 'Thank you,' and pulled a picture of [now 7-month-old] Pamela out of his wallet to show the guy. And the man said, 'Oh, I was talking about winning Rookie of the Year.'"

Laurie Urlacher is filling a trunk with mementos of Brian's career for Pamela, and there is one thing she treasures as much as any of the awards. It is a photograph of Brian and Pamela that ran in the *Tribune* last spring. Someone had clipped it and sent it to the Urlachers with no name or return address, just a note that reads, "No matter what you ever do on the field, this is the picture of a real man."

It is, at the very least, a picture of a contented man.

"Everything's in order now," he says, measurably more relaxed in demeanor than he was as a rookie. "A year ago at this time, we weren't even in our house yet and I was worried about my wife and brother [Casey, who lives with them] getting up here. Every day I was calling home and there was some other thing to worry about. Now everything is good at home and it's so much better."

Caravans of golf carts drive by and the players driving them give Urlacher a hard time as he is being interviewed, but he laughs easily and teases back. "Last year I felt really uncomfortable because every day in practice I had a bad day and everyone [in the media] still wanted to talk to me," he says. "That was really hard for me. Now it's OK. It's all good."

Bears coaches couldn't agree more.

"He'll be better this season because he understands what he's doing better," Blache says. "He understood football before, but when you get to the nuances, certain coverages, there were plays that he missed last year that he'll make this year.

"There was a pass for a touchdown in the Colts game where he just missed tipping the ball because he took three steps wrong. Had he not taken any steps wrong, he'd have intercepted it. There was also one in the New England game.

"There were two or three interceptions last year he didn't get that he'll get this season because he understands exactly where he fits in the scheme of things."

Bears coach Dick Jauron concurs. "I think he can be much better. A lot of it will be a function of how much better we are.

"A real good player on a not-very-good team is still good, but a real good player on a real good team, those guys look awfully good," Jauron says. "And they help everybody around them too. As we get better, I think he'll just get better and better."

The honors Urlacher picked up last year—most notably his Pro Bowl selection and consensus defensive Rookie of the Year award—did more than fill Pamela's trunk. They also contributed to an off-season tour of the U.S. the family has trouble keeping straight.

To their best recollection, the Urlachers went from Hawaii for the Pro Bowl to Los Angeles for a television interview, to New Orleans for an autograph signing session, to Albuquerque to visit friends and then to Lovington, N.M., to have Brian's high school jersey retired, to Washington, D.C., for the Unsung Hero Award voted upon by NFL players, back to Albuquerque for a friend's wedding, to Jamaica for the Superstar Challenge, to Atlanta for a charity golf outing, back to Albuquerque for his football camp, to Virginia to speak at the NFL's rookie symposium, then home to Lake Bluff for three weeks before he had to report to Platteville.

In between, Urlacher attended mini-camps in Lake Forest and got used to the idea of seeing himself on the side of CTA buses on posters that read, "The CTA eliminates long drives. So does he."

"I'll say to him, 'Isn't it weird to look around and see everyone wearing your jersey?' and he'll say, 'Uh, yeah,' but he barely notices," Laurie Urlacher says. "I told him, 'You need to sit back and let it soak in once in a while, Brian. I'll bet you never thought you'd be on the side of a bus in Chicago.'

"Someone called him recently and rattled off every single award he had received and asked him what was the most special thing that happened, and he answered, 'The birth of my daughter.' That's Brian."

Jauron says Urlacher's attitude is exactly what he wants in a leader and that the second-year linebacker is not too young to exert his influence. Urlacher, however, isn't so sure. "We have enough guys talking enough junk that I don't have to," he says.

He does allow that he'll be less tolerant of failure this year. "We expect to win this year," he says. "It just seems like we're so much further ahead in camp."

There is another motive as well. "We want to keep the coaches here," Urlacher says. "Everyone is saying if we don't win this year, [Jauron] will be out of here, so we take that as an incentive to win games.

"At least I do."

In the meantime, he stalks the field with his smile firmly in place. Not exactly the image of Dick Butkus, for whom the closest thing to a smile was a snarl, but an image Bears fans have already grown to appreciate.

"I'm glad the media covered him smiling that way because that was him—he truly enjoys it," Laurie Urlacher says. "Yes, money is nice. It makes life more comfortable. But it makes me happier to know that he'd still be doing this if he was making $25,000 a year. And that he'd still love it."

# Through Urlacher's Eyes

BY MELISSA ISAACSON

**Snapshots of a play.**

Phillip Daniels: "That's too much, that's too much."

Warrick Holdman: "That call [stunk]."

Walt Harris: "Come on, Big-Time."

Mike Brown: "Brian, hey, Golden Boy, you were supposed to be there."

Bryan Robinson: "Excuse me, but can you please give us the call?"

Brian Urlacher: "Listen."

That's all it takes to silence the Bears' defensive huddle. One word. To the point. And, for the next couple of seconds, anyway, calm is restored.

Anyone who has ever played NFL football struggles to describe what it's like to be on the field in the middle of it all, to put the controlled chaos into everyday terms. "To me," Bears linebacker Warrick Holdman says, "it's like the first time I went to downtown Chicago. I was walking, trying to find the Water Tower, and I was getting bumped, everyone was rushing past me and it was just confusing. On the field it's like that, but it's organized confusion."

Bears defensive coordinator Greg Blache says he would envision it like being inside a washing machine "in full cycle with soap, water, things flying, agitation up and down, the most utter chaos you've ever seen in your life."

It is a blur for those who never really cut it. It is manageable for those who do. It is a frame-by-frame series of snapshots for those who do it exceptionally well.

Through the eyes of middle linebacker Brian Urlacher, one play during the Bears' 17-10 victory over the Minnesota Vikings earlier this season provides a glimpse of how utter chaos breaks down to 45 seconds of looking, listening, planning, evaluating and reacting. It reveals how, in a span of five seconds, barely enough time for most of us to scratch our heads, Urlacher and his teammates have done all of those things and done them in concert.

## Getting Started

For Urlacher, an island of calm in the sea of madness, the play begins where the last one ends, his eyes immediately locating Blache among the maze of people on the sideline as he jogs to the

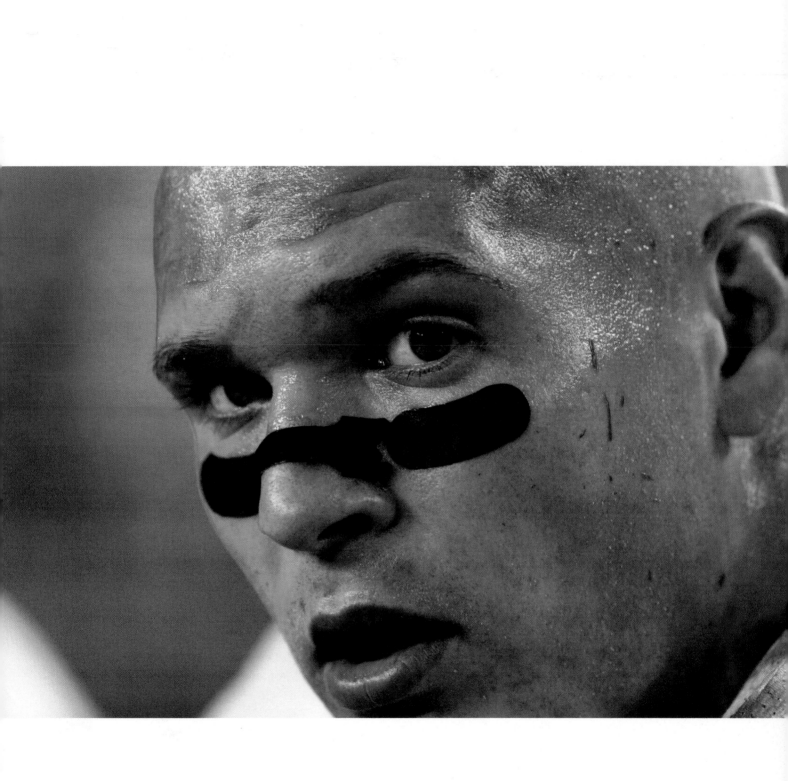

huddle. Last year Blache had to wear orange gloves to catch Urlacher's eye. This season Urlacher finds him immediately, standing on the new line of scrimmage.

At the same time, safeties Mike Brown and Tony Parrish are getting the down and distance from assistant defensive line coach Steve Little. And Holdman and strong-side linebacker Rosevelt Colvin are getting personnel signals from defensive line coach Rex Norris—"Regular" on this play meaning two backs, one tight end and two wideouts—and relaying that information to Urlacher.

Meanwhile, defensive end Bryan Robinson is stalking impatiently. "One of the things that irks me about Brian," Robinson says with a laugh, "is that he'll know the huddle call and we'll be sitting out there during the timeout and I'll say, 'Did he give you the call?' And he goes, 'Yeah, I got the call.' And I'm like, 'Well, give it to me so I can get it in my mind, know what I'm going to do.'"

"Oh, yeah," Urlacher says. "Yeah, B-Rob, I got it. Listen."

It's the cue to shut up and look up. One word: Listen. "Over-automatic, ready, break," Urlacher barks, telling his teammates the offensive front is swung to the tight end's side, the strong side. "Over" is his message to the defensive line and linebackers, telling them how to line up. "Automatic" is for the linebackers and secondary, telling them the coverage they want is based on the opponent's I-formation. That call has other calls built in, depending on what the Vikings do.

"It's great this year because once I hear something it's just a snap in my head and I know what to do," Urlacher says. "Last year it was like, 'Uhhh, OK, what does this mean again?' Then I'd process it. Now it's just second nature. One thought."

And that thought is often the same as Blache's. "It's scary," Blache says. "From the beginning we were on the same wavelength. He would finish things before I could say them. He'd be turning away [toward the huddle] and I'd say, 'Not so fast.' I feel very comfortable, very confident, even in the no-huddle situation when things are happening fast, that I can give him just the flicker and he's got it."

## The Huddle

The Bears use a square huddle—Urlacher's back is to the offense, and they huddle up in assigned places reflective of their positions on the field to facilitate communication and to expedite getting out of the huddle.

Once they break, Urlacher's real work begins. Locating the tight end first tells him his strength call—"Liz" for left, "Rip" for right. In this case it's "Liz," given in a hand signal that tells cornerbacks Walt Harris and R.W. McQuarters to line up on opposite sides of the field, strong safety Parrish to go left and free safety Brown to go right. With the same call, Colvin knows to go right, opposite the tight end, and Holdman goes left of the tight end.

Left tackle Ted Washington is on the center, as is generally the case, while right tackle Keith Traylor will be over the guard on the tight end's side. Daniels, the right end, and Robinson, the left end, are the only two who stay on their respective sides, regardless of Urlacher's strength call.

There is no small talk at this point. "We try to always use one-syllable words, preferably three-letter buzzwords for something else, just to make it as quick and simple as possible," linebackers coach Dale Lindsey says. "We don't have time for anything else."

But there's time for last-second warnings and reminders. "Rosie, watch flow, watch lead weak," Urlacher yells, cautioning Colvin to be aware that the fullback and tailback are on the tight end side, putting four receivers on one side.

In the secondary, similar exchanges are taking place.

"It's important, whether they know it or not, just to reinforce certain things," Parrish says. "The light might come on with someone or maybe there's a little tip he just remembered because you said something. Mike Brown and I are at the point now where I can just say his name and not even look at him and we know exactly what's going on."

Now the defensive linemen are yelling "Blue-I" or "Red-I," referring to which side the fullback is on and where the tailback is, in this case directly behind the quarterback.

There are two coverages the Bears can play in "Over-automatic." In this case, with this formation, Urlacher chooses "Cover three," which means three defensive backs playing deep with the three linebackers and the other corner playing underneath, in a zone.

If Urlacher blows the call—he did so only twice last season, leading to one big gain, and hasn't done it since—the defense knows what to do. "If I screw up, we're all screwed up together," he says. "As long as we're on the same page, doing the same thing, we're OK."

No one corrects him, even if they know he's wrong. Too confusing. Too many voices. But again, that is rarely necessary. "His percentage, even as a rookie, was better than anybody I've ever worked with," Blache says. "His percentage has been astronomical from day one."

## Find the Stars

Urlacher takes a quick look at the offense and looks for the featured players. "When you play the Vikings," he explains, "you always want to know where [Randy] Moss is."

Then he tries to cheat. "You can usually pick stuff off linemen. Sometimes they lean, sometimes they sit back in their stance or don't put their hand down, which means they're going to pass. And sometimes it doesn't work at all.

"I try to look at the backs' eyes sometimes, but obviously they're not stupid. They're not going to give themselves away. Or sometimes you can hear the quarterback calling out, 'White 20,' and then you know what to expect because he's done it before and you knew what play came after that."

If a Viking goes in motion, it's up to Urlacher to make checks or adjustments in the alignment, with Brown telling his fellow defensive backs and the linebackers whether to change coverages. A call like "Ram" or "Pinch" is a stunt call telling linemen to go to a different gap on the snap.

As if there isn't enough dialogue going in, coach Dick Jauron may well be calling in something from the sideline. "I might say, 'Watch the hard count, watch the bootleg, watch the screen'—very general terms," Jauron says.

## The Play Begins

If life is complicated before the snap, at least everyone is standing still. Once the play begins, "My mind is racing—what are they going to run out of this?" Urlacher says. "They're a big lead-weak team [running their lead blocker away from the tight end], so I'm thinking, 'Lean to my right on this play,' which is right at me. Then after you figure out what you'll do on the pass, you've got to know what you're doing on run. I hate play-action."

In this case the Vikings run play-action, which means the defense must determine if it's run or pass as quickly as possible. Literally within a second, Urlacher has it correctly figured as a pass, based on the movement of the linemen [they stand] and the path of the fullback, and with his back foot already planted—prepared for run or pass—he starts moving backward.

Locating the tight end, Urlacher watches to see if he crosses the field, which tells him to stay in the middle and find the primary receiver. "And he has to do all this in about two seconds," Lindsey says.

With his back to the quarterback, Urlacher now sees Cris Carter and determines he's going deep, so he immediately locates Moss coming across the middle and plays him man-to-man. "This was about a half-second," Lindsey says.

With Moss covered, quarterback Daunte Culpepper scrambles, with Robinson in hot pursuit. The play will end up with Culpepper, perhaps the most mobile quarterback in the league, gaining four yards.

Although he's tempted to go get Culpepper, Urlacher stays on Moss until the quarterback breaks the line of scrimmage. "If he goes up too soon, then Culpepper will lob it over his head and that's the bigger gain," Lindsey says.

"I'm always tempted," Urlacher says. "But I did that earlier in the game and they hit one over me."

## "Vision" and More

Told his stare seems fixed compared with the ever-darting eyes of Mike Singletary, Urlacher responds without hesitation, "Good periph, man," referring to his peripheral vision. "I can pretty much see the whole formation looking straight ahead."

His straight-ahead vision isn't bad either. "My wife had Lasik surgery and I have better vision than she does," he says. "I can see the last line on the eye chart. I'm a pretty lucky dude."

Combine that with his speed and he's more than lucky. Lindsey makes a comparison with Junior Seau, the San Diego Chargers' perennial All-Pro. "The difference between Brian and an average player, and it's the same with Seau, is that Brian is so quick he can screw up and still go make a play that the normal guy couldn't make if he hadn't screwed up," Lindsey says. "It's called acceleration and burst."

Reaction time also helps with a group that doesn't mind letting a teammate know in the most indelicate way that he has made a mistake. "You have to be quick with your comebacks," Urlacher says, laughing.

In that department he's not quite All-Pro caliber yet. "Everyone gets on Brian," Brown says. "He's an easy target because he's not real witty with his comebacks. He just says, 'Shut up.'"

Of course, Urlacher doesn't have to say, "Shut up."

Just, "Listen."

# Butkus on Urlacher

**BY RICK MORRISSEY**

**The world is heavily populated** with middle linebackers who were supposed to be The Next Dick Butkus. They fell away, one by one, lacking either Butkus's ability to inflict pain or his glee in doing it.

*Sports Illustrated* once offered up a perfect example of the rage that drove Butkus. While he was practicing one day as a player on Chicago Vocational High School's football team, he noticed that four boys in a car were harassing his girlfriend. Enraged, he ran across the field. The driver was no dummy—you see a maniac in full football gear headed your way, you know to take off—but his car lacked the necessary pick-up. Butkus sprinted down 87th Street, dived through the open window on the passenger's side and beat the brazenness out of each of them. You can't teach an open-road tackle.

This leads us to some good news for Bears fans. Butkus is starting to see a little of himself in Bears linebacker Brian Urlacher, and that's saying something. The First Dick Butkus has been hearing about The Next Dick Butkus for about 30 years, and he's tired of it. It's not that he believes today's players are unworthy of undoing his chin strap, it's that he doesn't have much use for comparisons.

But Urlacher is different. The Bears head into their biggest game in years Sunday at Green Bay with a middle linebacker who is beginning to dispense pain to opposing ballcarriers in large doses. Speed never has been an issue with Urlacher. But the great ones have played with abandon and anger, and there has been some question of whether Urlacher had the stomach for the requisite nastiness.

Butkus first noticed a change in Urlacher in the Minnesota game two weeks ago when the middle linebacker hit Vikings running back Doug Chapman in the backfield. Butkus saw a certain enjoyment in the meting out of justice. Urlacher hit Chapman hard and kept going. Afterward, Chapman resembled a puddle of purple on the Metrodome's artificial turf.

"That was my beef about him earlier," Butkus said of Urlacher. "To me, it seemed like he didn't run through the tackle. He doesn't punish the runner. He used to just grab them and fall

down. That was the first game where it really seemed to me he was running through ball carriers. With that speed, he can really hurt somebody. Now you're really going to be the old Monsters of the Midway. Just grabbing people and falling down is not going to get it."

Butkus would get ready for games by working himself into a lather. He was an anger-mismanagement class of one. He would see an opposing player laughing during warmups and convince himself that he was the object of ridicule.

That's his advice to Urlacher. Get mad. Actually, what Butkus said was that Urlacher needs to get "a wild hair" in a very sensitive area. And that he needed to stop helping people up after a tackle.

"Quit shaking hands and patting everybody on the back," Butkus said. "For an hour, he has to start labeling people. Once you start hitting people, now you have people thinking about it. Who knows? Somewhere along the line, they get worried about getting hit and all of a sudden they forget about holding on to the ball. And you have a turnover, maybe.

"If he can develop the punishment factor, some of these running backs have a tendency to chicken out when the going gets tough."

Urlacher has the talent to be a Pro Bowl selection for the next 10 years. In a dull game against Detroit last week, he had double-digit tackles again and went almost unnoticed. Maybe that's how we know how far he has come: There was no one play last week where he detonated an opposing ball carrier, no one play where he wrote his signature in black and blue. We've come to expect big plays from Urlacher.

That's what Chicago expected from Butkus, that and a decent blood flow. He still growls more than talks, as if he had slept the wrong way.

If you want to tell him that, in his prime, he wasn't fast enough to play in today's NFL, go right ahead. But I would recommend making sure the car is going at least 30 mph before you tell him.

"Right away people will say the speed of the game is different," Butkus said. "[Washington coach] Marty Schottenheimer is a good friend of mine. He says, 'Boy, these people are so fast. I don't know if you could play today.' I just say, 'I think I could find me a spot.'"

I believe he could.

# What a Catch!

**BY JOSEPH WHITE**

**When the fake field goal** was practiced two days before the game, Brian Urlacher dropped holder Brad Maynard's pass both times. Not surprisingly, teammates were having doubts about this particular trick play.

"Surely, he's not going to miss a third," Maynard said.

The third attempt was for real, in the fourth quarter with Chicago trailing by three points. Urlacher went in motion, and Maynard rolled right and found the linebacker wide open for a 27-yard touchdown, lifting the Bears to a 20-15 victory over the Washington Redskins on Sunday.

"When I saw him go in motion," linebacker Warrick Holdman said. "I was like, 'Oh, man!' because during practice it wasn't quite working right."

But Urlacher's first NFL reception was a clean catch, followed by a sprint to the goal line. He didn't even bobble it.

"In the game, I don't drop them," Urlacher said. "And that's all that matters."

And, once he scored, Urlacher gave the ball to kicker Paul Edinger for the spike.

"I don't like to spike," Urlacher said. "I don't do that stuff. I don't know what to do when I score."

Urlacher does know how to tackle—he led the team with eight solos and one assist—and the Bears (11-3) definitely know how to win. The victory added to a memorable season that includes come-from-behind overtime victories over San Francisco and Cleveland and a fourth-quarter comeback against Detroit.

Believe it or not, Urlacher isn't the first linebacker to catch a pass to beat Washington. Dick Butkus's reception in an aborted extra point was the difference in a 16-15 victory in 1971.

# Lone Defensive Pro Bowl Pick

**BY RICK GANO**

**Brian Urlacher is going back** to the Pro Bowl, but he won't see any of his defensive teammates from the Chicago Bears in Hawaii.

Even though the Bears have been the toughest NFL team to score on through 15 games, Urlacher was the only Chicago defensive player to be chosen to the NFC squad.

The Bears did get three other players selected later—offensive tackle James "Big Cat" Williams, center Olin Kreutz, and special teams standout Larry Whigham. It's the greatest number Chicago has had since four Bears were named for the 1992 game.

But with a defense that has intercepted 17 passes and recovered 17 fumbles and led the 12-3 team to within one win of a division title, the Bears expected more. Most noticeably absent was second-year safety Mike Brown.

Brown had five interceptions, including two for TDs to provide back-to-back overtime wins, forced two fumbles, and made three sacks.

"The best player on our team didn't even go," Urlacher said. "Mike Brown didn't even make it. I think most everyone on the team thinks he should be there."

Urlacher, who played in the Pro Bowl last year as a rookie after being selected as an alternate, leads the Bears with 131 tackles. He also has three interceptions, five sacks and has scored two touchdowns—one on a 90-yard fumble recovery and another on a pass off of a fake field goal.

"He's got exceptional athletic ability and exceptional smartness," defensive coordinator Greg Blache said. "Brian's the whole package.

"I think we had some other guys who were deserving. But there's a lot of popularity involved in the voting there, so it doesn't shock me. But we are somewhat disappointed."

# Sega Superstar

**Sega sports announced** in May 2002 that Brian Urlacher had signed on as their official spokesperson and cover athlete for the game "SEGA Sports NFL 2K3."

Urlacher helped design his character's moves during a session in which he wore a special suit to help game designers capture his signature moves. He also spent time in the studio recording defensive huddle audio calls, and he worked with the game's development team on designing defensive plays.

# Mama's Boy

**Urlacher and his mother,** Lavoyda, meet a group of school children during the filming of their commercial for Campbell's Chunky soup.

Urlacher is new to the "Mama's Boys" campaign, which also features NFL starts Donovan McNabb, Michael Strahan, and Jerome Bettis. The campaign debuts in September 2002.

# Honoring His Past

BY THE ASSOCIATED PRESS

Bears linebacker Brian Urlacher has demonstrated how much weight he gives the Lovington High School football program for helping make him a pro.

Hammer Strength personnel recently delivered a 38-piece weight-training package to the school's field house.

In all, Urlacher donated $40,000 worth of weight training equipment.

"I was happy to make this equipment donation. Lovington helped shape my football career," said Urlacher, a 1996 graduate of Lovington High, "and hopefully this equipment will enhance the conditioning and performance of these young athletes."

The equipment included four iso-lateral machines, five squat racks, and three ground base jammers, among others.

"It's an awesome feeling to get $40,000 worth of equipment—the best money can buy," said Jaime Quinones, Urlacher's football trainer and coach. "It's going to make the conditioning building the best in the state."

Bryce Karger, Urlacher's athlete representative with Kauffman Sports, said Urlacher enjoyed helping the school.

"Brian has the ability to be able to help his high school and the people who helped him," Karger said. "He knows how important it was for him to have the weights to become an NFL player and live out his dreams. Anything he can do, he's willing to do."

Karger added, "We hope to keep adding on to the equipment . . . to make that facility a premier facility in the entire state."

Urlacher also has started a $25,000 scholarship fund.

# Story Credits

"Versatile Throwback," by Pete Herrera, courtesy of the Associated Press. Page 8

"Linebacker Legacy" by the Associated Press. Page 16

"From Lovington to Loving Life" by Melissa Isaacson, courtesy of the *Chicago Tribune*. Copyrighted April 24, 2000, Chicago Tribune Company. All rights reserved. Used with permission. Page 22

"Signed to Five-Year Deal" by the Associated Press. Page 34

"Loses Starting Job" by the Associated Press. Page 40

"Interception Preserves Win" by the Associated Press. Page 46

"Surprised at Special Teams Honor" by Nancy Armour, courtesy of the Associated Press. Page 52

"Not Caught Up in the Hype" by Nancy Armour, courtesy of the Associated Press. Page 58

"Winning Top Rookie Honors" by Nancy Armour, courtesy of the Associated Press. Page 66

"Homecoming King" by Melissa Isaacson, courtesy of the *Chicago Tribune*. Copyrighted February 12, 2001, Chicago Tribune Company. All rights reserved. Used with permission. Page 74

"The Time of His Life" by Melissa Isaacson, courtesy of the *Chicago Tribune*. Copyrighted August 1, 2001, Chicago Tribune Company. All rights reserved. Used with permission. Page 84

"Through Urlacher's Eyes" by Melissa Isaacson, courtesy of the *Chicago Tribune*. Copyrighted October 19, 2001, Chicago Tribune Company. All rights reserved. Used with permission. Page 92

"Butkus on Urlacher" by Rick Morrissey, courtesy of the *Chicago Tribune*. Copyrighted December 9, 2001, Chicago Tribune Company. All rights reserved. Used with permission. Page 102

"What a Catch!" by Joseph White, courtesy of the Associated Press. Page 110

"Lone Defensive Pro Bowl Pick" by Rick Gano, courtesy of the Associated Press. Page 116

"Honoring His Past" by the Associated Press. Page 124

# Photo Credits

**Photos courtesy of Getty Images**
Al Bello, pages 1, 41
Chris Covatta, page 9
Jonathan Daniel, pages 12, 14, 18, 25, 31, 32, 36, 44, 48, 50, 54, 56, 62, 64, 69, 70, 72, 80, 82, 88, 100, 103, 106, 112, 114, 117, 120
Jed Jacobsohn, page 118
Andy Lyons, page 108
Mark Lyons, page 98
Doug Pensinger, page 125

**Photos courtesy of NFL Photos**
Allen Kee, page 105
Al Messerschmidt, pages 59, 85, 90, 93
Louis Raynor, page 1
Tony Tomsic, page 1

**Photos courtesy of UPI Photo Service**
Jim Bolt, page 35
Mark Cowan, page 53
Frank Polich, pages 38, 87

**Photos courtesy of Reuters**
Gary Cameron, pages 47, 97
Sue Ogrocki, pages 27, 88
Joe Skipper, page 60

**Photos courtesy of The Associated Press**
Stephen J. Carerra, page 67
Ric Feld, page 95
Fred Jewell, page 23
Seth Perlman, page 6
Jake Schoellkopf, page 11

Susan Walsh, page 111
Ted S. Warren, page 127
Nick Wass, page 20

**Photos courtesy of KRT Sports**
Candice C. Cusic, pages 75, 76, 79
Phil Velasquez, page 17

Photo courtesy of PR Newswire Photo Service, page 123

Photo courtesy of Sega Sports, page 122

All photos used with permission.

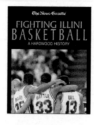
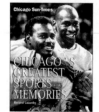

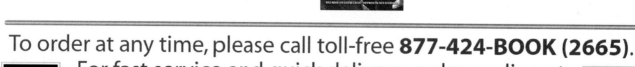